CAN CHANGE
YOUR DESTINY

Other Highland Books

FAITH CAN CHANGE YOUR DESTINY

by

BENSON IDAHOSA

HIGHLAND BOOKS

Printed in Great Britain for
HIGHLAND BOOKS
6 The White House, Beacon Road,
Crowborough, East Sussex TN6 1AB,
by Richard Clay (The Chaucer Press) Ltd, Bungay, Suffolk
Typeset by Nuprint Services Ltd, Harpenden, Herts AL5 4SE.

CONTENTS

FOREWORD

Many Christians are strangers to the idea of a living faith that expects God to intervene and change circumstances. They accept whatever happens to them with resignation, even imagining that such an attitude is a godly response to difficulty and need.

Benson Idahosa is a man who believes that Jesus came to reveal a God of intervention, one who in love for His children is concerned about their situation and desires to meet with them in every need, ready to change the circumstances whenever necessary—and whenever faith operates!

Like all men of true faith he does not theorise on the subject but points to the evidence of personal experience, where the biblical principles of faith have been worked out in practice. Such principles are learned in the hard experiences of the school of life. A man with a living faith meets difficulty with the truth of God's power made available through Jesus Christ.

That dimension of faith is the possession, potentially, of every believer. Dr Idahosa helps the reader to see how he can shape his destiny through trust in God rather than in his circumstances. Using the theme of the healing of blind Bartimaeus he brings home the truth that faith in Jesus actually works. There is no way of pleasing Him without faith and He loves to reward those who put their trust in Him.

Benson Idahosa's amazing ministry is a testimony to the fact that the principles he teaches work in experience. These principles will work in your life, for that same Lord and His Word are available to you.

Colin Urquhart

AUTHOR'S PREFACE: THE FAITH FACTOR

A prominent Bible scholar once said: 'Take from a man his wealth and you hinder him; take from him his faith and hope and you stop him.' 'Without faith it is impossible to please God,' in fact without it you cannot walk with Him. If without faith you cannot please Him—therefore please Him by your faith in Him and in His words.

To believe there is a Supreme Being who created heaven and earth is one thing. To believe and place faith in Him to reign and rule in your life is another issue. That is where your faith comes in. That is trusting God to bring you to life's highest point.

Faith is the active force which draws the thin line between success and failure. Faith in God through Christ declares, 'He shall bring you to a successful end.'

E. W. Kenyon said, 'What you have undeveloped in you has no value.' This book will show you how I placed value on my faith and saw the emergence of a new man, unwilling to yield to tradition and formalism. Faith in God changed my destiny, touching millions all around the world.

I say to you, 'Arise in your faith.' I have placed in your

hands the secret; it worked for me—God can make it work for you too.

HAVE FAITH IN GOD!

Archbishop Benson A. Idahosa

Chapter One

THE SUBSTANCE OF FAITH

*Faith comes from hearing the message, and the
message is heard through the word of Christ*

Romans 10:17

The issue of faith among Christians through the ages has always attracted speculation, tending sometimes to unbelief and often to wrong understanding and application of God's Word on the subject. This has resulted in confusion and doubt. Whatever position a Christian may find himself in, a good understanding, appreciation and application of faith in the walk with God will make a lot of difference; his attitude to faith will determine whether he is fulfilled or frustrated. Faith is recognised as a vital ingredient in the Christian recipe.

As a Gospel preacher who has spoken to thousands on every area of human endeavour, I realise that faith is the moving force that takes God's Word for what it says. This is important! How many times a day can one pray? Once, twice, three times? 'As many times as possible', you may say. Great! The Bible does not specify how many times a Christian *ought* to pray, but recommends unceasing prayer. Do you pray with folded hands? Surely that is a defeatist position. But whatever physical attitude is adopted, the confessing prayer by a believer must be acted upon by faith. I am not talking about prayers uttered at religious ceremonies; I have in mind what is called 'the prayer of faith'.

You may have excellent physical vision, yet be spiritually

blind. The Bible says we have two sets of eyes: physical eyes and eyes in our soul. The eyes in our soul have been blinded by Satan if we fail to operate by faith. 'But if our gospel be hid, it is hid to them that are lost; In whom the god of this world hath blinded the minds of them which believe not, lest the light of the glorious gospel of Christ, who is the image of God, should shine into them' (2 Cor 4:3–5). The Gospel and its promises are hidden from the lost. As believers or born-again Christians we can therefore pray, '...the eyes of your understanding being enlightened; that ye may know what is the hope of his calling, and what the riches of the glory of his inheritance in the saints' (Eph 1:17–18).

But facing the facts as they stand, there are many post-Christian doubters, seemingly incapable of standing upon the Master's Word. Is it *really* true?' they sneer. Bible truths stand sure, with deeper foundations than we can comprehend, 'for the Word of God will never pass away' (Mat 24:35). I have often meditated on Hebrews 11:6 which states: 'But without faith it is impossible to please him, for he that cometh to God must believe he is, and that he is a rewarder of them that diligently seek him.' What makes it impossible to please God? The unceasing answer, from before the past and until after the future, is lack of faith.

Bartimaeus had faith to win

Faith is the bricks and mortar with which we must build our relationship with God and our glorious hope for eternity. The story of blind Bartimaeus gives considerable food for thought, and above all offers sublime lessons for the Christian walk in faith. Let us take a careful look at the story in Mark 10:46–52.

Every morning Bartimaeus would beg from the people who passed by, 'Help the blind! Help the blind! Help the blind!' Once in a while someone tossed a coin to him. Some cruel, hard-hearted people spat on him. They abused and laughed him to scorn, 'Get away from here!' Surely blind Bartimaeus hoped and longed for a change in his degrading circumstances? Do you not think that the more they laughed him to scorn the more his faith grew for change? I believe so.

Bartimaeus was helpless, blind and poor, only to be pitied, or so it seemed. But one day a message had come to him, and he had never forgotten it. Someone had told him about Jesus of Nazareth, Who could heal. True Christian faith rests on the specific content of belief: it is not a vague thing which takes the place of real understanding. Blind Bartimaeus sincerely believed in the healing power of Jesus Christ and sat quietly listening to each new account of the exploits of Jesus in nearby towns. He thought to himself, 'Jesus would never come to a town like Jericho. If only he would . . . .' And from this multitude of tiny choices, unrelated circumstances, unnoticed influences, we too shape the strength and substance of our faith, in preparation for a necessary change.

Hebrews 11:1 presents a truth which is foundational to all aspects of faith: 'Now faith is the substance of things hoped for, the evidence of things not seen'. Bartimaeus first of all believed with all his heart in the works of Jesus Christ—'How God anointed Jesus of Nazareth with the Holy Ghost and with power: who went about doing good, and healing all that were oppressed of the devil; for God was with him' (Acts 10:38). Bartimaeus had implicit faith in Christ as a person and looked forward to receiving his healing through Him. Bartimaeus had never seen Jesus but believed His works as true: 'And being fully persuaded that what He had promised, He was able also to perform' (Rom 4:21).

What can you say of 'the evidence of things not seen' (Heb 11:1b)? Bartimaeus acted upon his faith in Jesus and 'called those things which be not as though they were' (Rom 4:17b). Does that not sound like an evidence of things not seen? On this morning as he staggered along in his tattered robe he heard a crowd of people down the road. He sensed that something important was happening although, of course, he could not see a thing. 'Who's coming? What's happening?' he asked anxiously, only to be met with indifference and rejection.

It was all too much for blind Bartimaeus. And as the crowd was beginning to move past, he reached out in desperation and frenzy and grabbed hold of someone. 'What's happening?' he asked, with anger and self-pity. As the man pulled away, he barked back at Bartimaeus, 'Jesus of Nazareth is passing by.' The drama that followed was to change Bartimaeus' life forever. 'Jesus of Nazareth! That's the great teacher I have heard about, who can heal!' he might have pondered momentarily. The Bible says faith comes by hearing the Word of God (Rom 10:17). Blind Bartimaeus had heard about Jesus and believed in Him, and in the twinkling of an eye his mind recaptured and assembled all known information on Jesus' ministry. That was the solid rock upon which he stood by faith, 'the substance of things hoped for' (Heb 11:1a).

Faith believes

The faith factor in the Christian walk is delicate and crucial and deserves detailed study until it is clearly understood. This is not only because, without it, it's 'impossible to please God' but also because God has given to 'every man the measure of faith' (Rom 12:3b). It is saddening to hear such exclamations as, 'I cannot believe that, it is impossible, God cannot do it.' Many dejected millions have put their faith, even their measure of faith, in something other than God. What does the Scripture say? 'It is better to trust in the Lord, than to put confidence in man. It is better to trust in the Lord, than to put confidence in princes' (Ps 118:8–9).

The sad state of affairs today is that people put their trust in human institutions, science and knowledge; as all these come tumbling down like a pack of cards, their hope crumbles. But 'Jesus Christ is the same yesterday, today and forever' (Heb 13:8). I have often pondered over Hebrews 11:6 and its words always hit me with great freshness and power—'without faith . . .' Conversely, we can assume that '*with* faith you *can* please God'. Lack of faith puts you out of line with God. It therefore stands to reason that faith places you in direct contact, in tune with Him. That sounds interesting, doesn't it? Pick up your Bible and read Hebrews 11:6 as you ask: 'What is required from him that cometh to God?' The answer: 'he must believe that *He is*.'

Faith believes in the great 'I AM'

How do we understand that 'I AM THAT I AM!' (Ex 3:14)? He is all that He says He is as revealed in His word (2 Tim 3:16, Heb 1:1–2). God says, 'I AM!' 'What and who is He?' you may dare to ask? And God says, 'I am that which I will show myself to be.'

'In the beginning God created the heavens and the earth' (Gen 1:1). What else? 'God created man in His own image. In the image of God created He him; male and female created He them' (Gen 1:27). What more? 'God, who at sundry times and in divers manners spake in time past unto the fathers by the prophets, Hath in these last days spoken unto us by His Son, whom he hath appointed heir of all things, by whom also He made the worlds.' (Heb 1:1–2). These are truths from the inspired Word of God which must, without question, be the substance of your walk of faith.

'Let us draw near with a true heart, in full assurance of faith . . . Let us hold fast the profession of our faith without wavering; for He is faithful that promises' (Heb 10:22–23). I have had the privilege of preaching Christ in many nations of the world and have met challenging situations that have put my faith in Jesus Christ under great strain, yet I always sense that this is the way to spiritual growth.

Faith put to the test

A while ago my wife and I were travelling by air from Sweden to the United States. We were 42,000 feet from the ground, and I was quietly thinking over the work that awaited us in America. I felt like taking a nap. But suddenly I heard the thunderous and panicky voice of the pilot announce, 'Ladies and gentlemen, I have been flying for thirty-two years, but this is the first time I have had to admit that I don't know where we are. If any of you knows how to pray, please do so.' There was an atmosphere of tension and uncertainty and a look of despair in every eye. But I knew God was in control.

Meanwhile pandemonium broke out; many passengers were very frightened. My mind raced home to our four children. The devil whispered, 'One of you should have been at home for the burial.' I quickly rebuked the thought and stood on the Word of God (Ps 50:15). My wife bowed her head and held my hand tight, speechless, and I could tell she was not praying! In the twinkling of an eye, I stood up in my seat against a background of wild stares from alarmed passengers. I spoke. 'Captain, in the name of Jesus, I am here. If you don't know where we are, I know. Jesus is the way, the truth and the life,' I continued seriously. 'I am on my way to America to preach, not to fall into the sea.' And as I sat down I heard a sighing 'Thank you Jesus', from my wife. I requested tea and the attendant shot back, 'Did you not hear the announcement?' 'Which one, mine?' I replied.

Suddenly the pilot's voice came on the air, 'I don't know what happened, but I know where we are!' There was clapping and cheers; certainly for my Lord Jesus Christ. My faith was in Christ and I shall always say, '. . . Yea, though I walk through the valley . . . I shall fear no evil' (Ps 23:4a).

The trials and the crises of life will surely come, but let

the substance of your faith be in Christ Jesus. God is not some indifferent force having a good time unmindful of His creation. Neither is He an abstract object without feeling or compassion for all you go through today. God has revealed Himself to you in several ways; each must be accepted by faith based upon your belief.

Does not creation——the firmament, the animals and nature itself——breathe upon you a wave of awe and bewilderment every time you look at it? Could you honestly say that your conscience does not nag you sometimes? Does not your conscience by God's inbuilt apparatus unceasingly bear testimony to the fact that there is an eternal Being, a supreme intelligence who keeps creation together with divine precision? I recollect a friend who, after a thoughtful look at the wonders of creation sighed, 'I can fight anything, but not my conscience; there is God,' (read Ps 14:1.)

The most comprehensive argument for creation is seen in the Bible and God's revealed plan for man's redemption through Jesus Christ: 'So then faith cometh by hearing, and hearing by the Word of God' (Rom 10:17).

Chapter Two

BELIEVING FAITH

Before they call I will answer; while they are still speaking I will hear.

Isaiah 65:24

In the minds of many people the issue of the credibility of Christianity has to do with the fact that Christianity requires an element of faith. Believe it or not, the word 'faith' produces goose pimples for millions of people. It makes them feel nervous, because 'faith' in our day is seen as a weird, hazy concept.

An aeroplane makes a forced landing after developing an engine fault and a knee-knocking passenger asks the smiling pilot, 'How did we pull through it all?' The pilot, with an air of self-confidence, may take a deep breath and reply, 'Well, we came through by faith.' Faith is not as vague a concept as many like to believe.

Listen carefully to what Pastor Charles Blair of Calvary Temple, Denver, has to say. Blair is a man of goals and faith in God. Each time he preaches he invites people to surrender their lives to Jesus Christ: 'Through all ages faith has been the test which God has given to every man' he says. 'It has always been required of man to believe that God, our heavenly Father, wants the very best for each of us. This is still very much the basis of God's dealing with us. Take the faith He has given you (Rom 12:36) and direct it back to Him and His promises, and watch it grow into a strong, towering, mountain-moving faith.' Do you see the difference? 'It is not our faith that saves; it is Christ who saves, but our faith is the connecting link,' according to Oswald J. Smith.

Man's belief must arise from something superior to him, mustn't it? Time and again I have had people from all walks of life crowd in on me asking for prayer. One point I have never failed to explain is the faith factor. Do you realise that prayer and faith are not gambling gadgets before God? Maybe you need to remember the words of social scientist Benjamin Kidd who, after considerable study and thought, stated, 'The world is governed much more by faith than it ever is by proven fact or knowledge.' Take a look at Hebrews 11:3. Faith makes a basic demand on every applicant who stands before God: that is, the belief that He is able to answer the prayer. The prophet Isaiah notes, 'And it shall come to pass that before they call, I will answer; and while they are yet speaking, I will hear' (Is 65:24).

Faith in action

In his book *Faith is for People* (Vision House, 1976) Paul Little, Director of Evangelism for Inter-Varsity Christian Fellowship, USA, makes some remarkable and revealing comments on this interesting subject. 'Now when we discuss this question of faith, there are three observations that we must keep in mind before we can discuss the question intelligently. The first observation is that *faith is no more valid than the object in which it is placed, whether that object is a person or a thing.*'

24

If the object of our faith is valid we have valid faith. If the object of our faith is invalid, we have nothing more than superstition. Let's think for a moment of a witch doctor in some primitive culture in the world. He prepares a brew that he gives to a desperately anxious father whose little daughter is seriously ill with a high fever. The father takes the potion to his daughter because he has intense faith and belief. He is very sincere but his sincerity does not save the life of his daughter if the witch doctor's potion happens to be poisonous. In this case the father's faith amounts to nothing more than superstition, since the object of his faith is invalid. The invalidity of faith is determined by its object and not by its intensity.

Pastor Paul Little deals with a second observation. 'This is the point: faith enables us to enter into the reality of that which is already true. Nor does lack of faith erase truth; what's true is still true. There's nothing spooky about the word faith. It simply means confident trust in something that is true.' And doesn't the Bible say 'Jesus is *the* way, *the* truth and *the* life . . .' (Jn 14:16)? And yet a third observation is that every one of us exercises faith every day we live. Faith is not something reserved for a particular type of emotionally-constructed person, faith is something that each of us exercises each day:

> The real question is not whether one person has faith and another person does not (since all of us have faith); the real question is whether the object of our faith is worth trusting when we are discussing the question. Is Christianity credible? We recognise that the object of one's Christian faith is Jesus Christ! Is Jesus Christ a valid object for my faith? Is He a trustworthy person? Is he someone to Whom I can commit myself with confidence?

I believe that He is. My decision is based on both external and internal evidence. External evidence has to do with undeniable living proofs of believing faith in the lives of millions of born-again, Spirit-filled believing Christians all over the globe (read Gal 2:20). Internal evidence concerns what the Scriptures say about believing faith and what comes out of it in individual lives.

Let us see what the Bible says in Mark 10:47: 'And when he heard that it was Jesus of Nazareth he began to cry out and say, Jesus, thou Son of David, have mercy on me.' Read over the above verse and you will notice a little misnomer in blind Bartimaeus' SOS appeal to Jesus on the Jericho road. Bartimaeus was blind and could not, therefore, have read from any scroll about Jesus of Nazareth being the Son of David. You believe with me that he merely heard of it from a good friend.

Faith stands upon God's words

If you read his words carefully you will conclude that even before the arrival of Jesus Christ, Bartimaeus had implicit faith that his confidence was in someone who could relieve him of his handicap. And the Word of God emphasises that 'whosoever shall call upon the name of the Lord shall be saved' (Rom 10:13). Are you not sure that blind Bartimaeus had this thought in mind? 'Jesus, save me!' he shouted, 'Jesus, please! Help me! Mercy! Mercy!' He was crying for exactly the right thing, mercy. Not only did he cry for the right thing, but he cried out at the right time. There was no time to waste, every minute counted. Jesus of Nazareth was passing by.

Blind Bartimaeus had a precious gift you need to pray for; the ability to deal with a specific thing at the correct time. The presence of believing faith in your life does not permit you to make vague requests before God. Many people have received no apparent answers to prayers because they have made this mistake. The Scriptures declare that, '. . . if two of you shall agree on earth as touching anything that they shall ask it shall be done for them of my Father which is in heaven.' Now with your believing faith in Christ, do the asking, mindful of exactly what you need, because there is even greater assurance in the Word: 'If thou canst believe, all things are possible to him that believeth' (Mk 9:23).

Faith in God brings a miracle

One afternoon in the early years of my ministry I and one of my converts stopped at my wife's house for a visit; we were not married then. We found the place full of her relations. There was agitation on every face, and many of the women were crying. 'What's going on?' I inquired. 'It's my uncle's baby', Margaret explained, wiping her tears with the back of her hand. 'She was ill for several days, and this morning she died. She kept having convulsions, but the local doctors could do nothing to help her. We even made sacrifices at the juju shrine here in our house, but she died anyway.'

'Where is the baby now?' I asked anxiously. 'There,' Margaret answered, gesturing toward the bedroom. 'We have already bathed the body and bought the coffin for her burial.' With feelings of righteous indignation burning within me, I turned to the father of the baby. 'The God I serve can bring your baby back to life,' I said confidently. 'Will you permit me to pray for her?' Startled, the father agreed, though he himself was not a Christian.

I walked boldly into the next room where the cold, still form of the baby lay on the bed. I ordered everyone out except my Christian companion, and closed the door. There was tension and expectation as the relations waited. Several minutes passed. Suddenly the startled family heard the baby sneeze. They rushed into the room to find the baby awake and looking completely normal. 'She is going to be all right,' I told the mother, who gathered the child in her arms. 'Give her something to eat,' I instructed as I walked out.

Margaret was deeply moved by the event, and felt shame for her previous mockery of the gospel. She had seen believing faith in Christ Jesus in action. 'Maybe there *is* something to what he's preaching, after all,' she thought. Your believing faith will affect people close to you, and will force them also to take a stand for Jesus. It is crucial that you stand upon the Word, maintain a position of unfluctuating belief in Christ and walk on to victory, always 'Looking unto Jesus, the author and finisher of our faith' (Heb 12:2).

The greatest weakness afflicting professing Christians today is lack of constancy in the Christian race. Bartimaeus did not allow his faith to waver. Jesus never came that way again. Jesus was on his way to Jerusalem to die. Reading between the lines you find out that if Bartimaeus had not met Jesus that day, he might never have received his sight; he might never have received forgiveness. What a startling thought!

28

Childlike belief in God's Word

Believing faith in Jesus Christ is honoured by God the Father, for it is written, 'If ye shall ask anything in my (Jesus') name, I will do it' (Jn 14:14), and the Apostle Paul tells us without one iota of doubt: '. . . God shall supply all your need, according to his riches in glory by Christ Jesus' (Phil 4:19). We should never forget this. The believing faith prayer that God honours is seen in all that our Lord Jesus Christ prayed. He prayed for you, with you, to God, and the prayer is answered because they were in agreement.

God does not go against His Word, 'For there is one mediator between God and men, the man Christ Jesus' (1 Tim 2:5). Yet today we hear amazing stories—of quacks who deceive many with unbelievably bizarre tales. What does the Bible say? What is the holy Word of the almighty God saying, if only men would read? The Bible speaks of Jesus in Hebrews 4:15, 16: 'For we have not an High Priest which cannot be touched with the feeling of our infirmities; but was in all points tempted as we are, yet without sin. Let us therefore come boldly unto the throne of grace, that we may obtain mercy and find grace to help in time of need.' God cares for our needs more than we can imagine. And He asks of you just one thing—believing faith in Jesus Christ.

Chapter Three

WALKING IN FAITH

Be faithful, even to the point of death, and I will give you the crown of life.

Revelation 2:10

The Bible weaves many beautiful illustrative stories of how you can stay in line with God, living a life of fruitfulness through simple faith in Jesus Christ; and we have already established a few fundamental truths in a walk of faith and dependence upon God through Jesus Christ Who is able to do even more than we ask. Standing upon the substance of faith and believing God in His totality brings you to the threshold of walking in faith. Essentially, success on this rather difficult ground depends on your in-depth understanding of God's word, His immutable promises concerning your life now and hereafter. Your heart will leap with joy to read in the gospel of Mark (chapter 10:29–30), '. . . There is no man that hath left house, or brethren, or sisters, or father, or mother, or wife or children, or lands, for my sake, and the gospel's, but he shall receive an hundred-fold now in this time . . . and in the life (world) to come eternal life.'

That is not all, for Paul wrote to the Corinthians (1 Cor 15:19), 'If in this life only we have hope in Christ, we are of all men most miserable.' But we thank God for Jesus Christ who assures us, 'Be thou faithful unto death, and I will give thee a crown of life' (Rev 2:10). 'Be thou faithful' speaks of a constancy and straight walking in faith, even unto death. Does that send shivers down your spine? There is no cause for alarm as long as you know who you are in God through Christ Jesus and the hope of His high calling.

Allow me to share a few inspiring verses of who you are before God, justified before Him, through Christ our Saviour. The Word of God says of you, 'For as many as are led by the Spirit of God, they are the sons of God' (Rom 8:14). Furthermore, 'The Spirit itself beareth witness with our spirit, that we are the children of God: And if children then heirs: heirs of God, and joint-heirs with Christ; if so be that we suffer with him that we may be also glorified together. For I reckon that the sufferings of this present time are not worthy to be compared with the glory which shall be revealed in us' (Rom 8:16–18).

Take time to study the great, living promises that God has made to you, a child of the kingdom. They will change your life as you act upon them by faith in Jesus Christ (Jn 6:63; Jn 14:12). Speak them right in the face of the devil—after all, he knows the Scriptures, doesn't he? Have you not read how our Lord Jesus Christ defeated the devil thrice with words of Scripture (Matt 4, Lk 4)? He thundered these words in the face of the devil: 'It is written, Man shall not live by bread alone, but by every word that proceedeth out of the mouth of God' (Matt 4:4). If Jesus Christ, even the Lord, needed the Word, then we certainly cannot risk leaving it out of our daily faith walk. After all, Christianity is not something that we use just in times of trouble. It is commitment to God that gives one meaning and purpose for all of life.

Hand in hand with Christ

Walking in faith in Jesus Christ will call sometimes upon all your reserves of energy and confidence in nothing else but Him. You know what? Jesus Christ calls you friends, brothers and sisters! And who is a friend? Someone who definitely knows the worst about us but still remains our friend. Sometimes I have had people ask me whether it is really possible to depend by faith on Jesus alone? And without hesitation I have always replied, 'Yes, absolutely.' In His own Word we read '. . . I will never leave thee nor forsake thee' (Heb 13:5).

The Christian walk has not in any way changed through the ages. The advance of technology has led many people to a position of dependence on the works of science. But there is no security in science. In all His work since creation, God has been unable to do without faith. Anything which works against faith hinders His purposes: 'Anything that is not of faith is sin.' Our perception of God's actions and his character are all based on faith, that is, 'you must believe that He is.'

God commanded Adam and Eve to 'be fruitful, and multiply, and replenish the earth, and subdue it . . .' (Gen 1:28). Only a God of faith could issue such a command. Adam and Eve believed and walked in faith to the redemption of this commandment. 'And Adam called his wife's name Eve, because she was the mother of all living' (Gen 3:20). God honours believing, walking faith and this produces a God-sent response to a specific need.

Faith in God brings fulfilment

There is so much truth in the story of Bartimaeus that I must return to it. Bartimaeus cried out to Jesus and there was immediate response, 'Jesus commanded him to be called' (Mk 10:49a). But did Blind Bartimaeus feel scared of Jesus and run away in the opposite direction? No, he got up, 'and casting away his garment, rose and came to Jesus' (Mk 10:50). Beloved, walking in faith with God through Jesus Christ demands your laying all else aside, 'every weight and the sin which doth so easily beset us' (Heb 12:1b). Bartimaeus ran to Jesus, and the Lord said, 'Your faith has made you whole'. Notice, not your intellectual understanding, not your money, not your works, but your faith. Faith! That's all it takes.

Look at the story of young David as he faces mighty and ungodly Goliath; read about the Samaritan woman in John 4; both were solely dependent on faith in God. Another man in the Bible faced a bleak future: he had no hope at all. 'And Jabez was more honourable than his brethren; and his mother called his name Jabez, saying, Because I bare him with sorrow' (1 Chron 4:9). Jabez put his faith in God. He rebelled against his situation of sorrow and anguish because he knew by faith that God had a worthwhile future in store for him. Praise God for His everlasting peace and compassion, for truly, 'The righteous cry, and the Lord heareth and delivereth them out of all their troubles' (Ps 34:17).

Did Jabez see God face to face? No, but he believed in His supremacy and God honoured his faith in Him: 'And Jabez called on the God of Israel saying, Oh that thou wouldest bless me indeed, and enlarge my coast . . . And

God granted him that which he requested' (1 Chron 4:10). And so the story goes. The faith of Jabez, placed in the God of Israel, changed his destiny for good. That is the plan of God for your life, brothers and sisters! put your faith in God through Christ the Lord, and don't give up. You can have faith to change your destiny, your business and your home, believing with Jabez that 'With God nothing shall be impossible' (Lk 1:37).

Faith elevates you

Some years ago, a young woman (who today is an energetic church minister) heard of my forthcoming crusade at the Stadium in Benin City, Nigeria. She hurriedly drove over to her friend on the other side of town to discuss this evangelistic outreach. Reluctantly, her friend agreed to accompany her to the crusade, and to Ogbe Stadium they came. God was in control and moving in their lives. After preaching a salvation message on repentance and forgiveness of sins through faith in Jesus Christ, I gave an altar-call. Lo and behold, my friend, along with many thousands of others, trooped to the altar in solemn response. Their lives have never been the same since: they have climbed from faith to faith, pressing on for Jesus. It is true that new faith has an effect on the quality of living; doubters take note!

A soap manufacturer who was a non-churchgoer walked down the street with a minister. 'The Gospel you preach has not done much good,' he said. 'The world is still filled with wickedness.' They passed a little girl making mud pies, and very much involved in her work. 'Soap has not done much good, would you say?' asked the minister, pointing to the child. 'It's useful only when applied,' said the manufacturer. 'Precisely!' said the minister.

Give Jesus Christ a chance, put all your faith in Him, walk in and with Him, and you will glimpse a new horizon.

Chapter Four

LIVING FAITH

I live by faith in the Son of God who loved me and gave himself for me.

Galatians 2:20

Now that we have examined the substance of faith and what it takes to have believing faith from day to day, we must think about some further questions. Where do we go from here? Where does faith lead? What is its end? These are important issues because our Christian life must be founded upon solid ground. This will make all the difference in counteracting the frustration which is the lot of many Christians. Living faith must contend with the great forces of the devil, as pointed out in 1 Peter 5:6–7. 'Humble yourselves therefore under the mighty hand of God, that he may exalt you in due time: Casting all your care upon him, for he careth for you. Be sober, be vigilant; because your adversary the devil, as a roaring lion, walketh about, seeking whom he may devour: whom resist steadfast in the *faith* . . .'

God calls for constant humility from His children as we 'abide under the shadow of the Almighty' (Ps 91:1). As you may have noticed from the verse, there is considerable emphasis on humility, for very good reasons. Humility distinguishes us from the devil, who could not humble himself before God but rebelled against Him. If you read Isaiah 14:12–15 and the five 'I wills' of Satan's fall, you will see why God calls for humility. Humility as a daily guide goes forth to the object of our faith, that is Jesus Christ, '... the author and finisher of our faith' (Heb 12:2). As exemplified in 1 Peter 5:9, we must resist the devil steadfastly in faith through Jesus Christ, and he will flee (Jas 4:7). Living faith will help us to weather the storms that so often beset us on life's voyage.

I recollect the refreshing words of the late Dr A. W. Tozer: 'Faith... is living through every circumstance of life with Almighty God in focus, to whom nothing is impossible.' Hallelujah! In the vivid words of Dr V. Raymond Edmon, 'Faith is dead to doubts, dumb to discouragements, blind to impossibilities, knows nothing but success.' It is essential that we who profess Christianity behave in accordance with the faith.

Fact, faith and feeling

Another avenue of evidence for living faith is described in this illustration by Paul Little from his book *Faith is for People*:

> You may have heard the old proverb of Mr Fact, Mr Faith and Mr Feeling. Mr Fact, Mr Faith and Mr Feeling were walking along a very narrow wall. As long as Mr Faith kept his eye on Mr Fact, Mr Feeling followed right along and they made beautiful progress. But every time Mr Faith turned around and looked at Mr Feeling, they almost fell off, because they were so paralysed with fear. They just crept along inch by inch out of mortal fear. The moral of the story is that our feelings will follow our faith in the facts. Our certainty of salvation rests in the fact of what God has done

for us in Jesus Christ and the fact of our personal commitment to Jesus Christ. If our faith lies in these facts, we find our feelings following along without difficulty.

This illustration makes simple some hard truths, as does the story of Bartimaeus. What an experience for him. What an experience to open one's eyes and look straight into the strong, tender face of Jesus! Then he saw the sunlight, the mountains of Moab, the palm trees and the walls of Jericho. Then people, and faces. He began to shout and jump up and down, and say, 'I can see! I can see!' We read in Mark 10:52 that after meeting Jesus, Bartimaeus *followed Jesus in the way*'. You receive Him today, and then you follow Him for a lifetime through a daily walk of consistent faith. Bartimaeus changed his destiny! What does the Lord say? 'I am the vine, ye are the branches. He that abideth in me and I in him, the same bringeth forth much fruit; for *without me ye can do nothing*' (Jn 15:5).

In his book *We would see Jesus*, Roy Hession wrote that God draws redeemed individuals into co-operation with Himself in the outworking of His glorious purposes and we become His branches on which His fruit is borne. Without God the branches can do nothing: without branches the vine does not bear fruit. We do not however, produce or initiate the fruit. That is altogether *His* work as we faithfully surrender to Him. I have time and again stressed that no believing Christian can accept Jesus Christ as personal Lord and Saviour, lay claim to salvation and new birth, and then go on to live a life based on anything else but faith. That would be absurd! The Word of God declares with clarity and intensity that, 'Therein is the righteousness of God revealed from faith to faith: as it is written, The just shall live by faith' (Rom 1:17, Hab 2:4; Heb 10:38; Gal 3:11).

Conversion is really only the entrance to a long pilgrimage, a pilgrimage that has mountain peaks, deep valleys, resting places—and even a few swamps; but praise His name, our unshakable confidence day by day is that from the fall of a raindrop to the fall of an empire, all is under the providential hand of God. To read His word on this point we must turn to Matthew 10:30–31, for 'the very hairs of your head are all numbered. Fear ye not therefore; ye are of more value than many sparrows' (Matt 10:30, 31).

When I was on a recent evangelistic trip aboard, a young man commented to me that 'the Christian's chief occupational hazards are depression and discouragement.' And just as he turned away, I said firmly, 'Faith is more than believing something, regardless of the consequences.'

Hall of faith

The Bible has a 'Hall of Faith,' which is carefully set out in Hebrews 11. It is sheer delight to read there about the all-time greats of the Bible—and eternity! Each was a man or woman of inimitable faith, in word and deed. Look at Enoch (Heb 11:5) whose life was changed by faith in God. It is heart-warming to read about the exploits of father Abraham, Moses, David and Abel. Have you noticed the account of Rahab? She believed God and her faith in Him changed her destiny; King David, and so our Lord Jesus Christ (Matt 1:5), were among her descendants.

There are a few vital pointers to guide us along the way of faith. The Reverend Wesley Nelson in his book, *Capti-*

vated by Christ, highlights the importance of prayer. 'Because prayer is revitalised through fellowship with Christ there is a tendency to look upon prayer as a way to Christ . . . The Bible witnesses to Christ and when Christ is near, the Bible is a new book.' Living faith in God through Jesus Christ needs to be firmly rooted in regular fellowship, Bible reading and unceasing prayers (Heb 10:25; Ps 119:105; Lk 18:1).

With a heart overflowing with His blessings, I share this timeless verse of Scripture with you: 'I am crucified with Christ: nevertheless, I live; yet not I, but Christ liveth in me: and the life I now live in the flesh, I live by the faith of the Son of God, who loved me, and gave himself for me' (Gal 2:20).

Chapter Five

LIFE-CHANGING FAITH

'Whatever you ask for in prayer, believe that you have received it, and it will be yours.'

Mark 11:24

Faith is a fascinating topic for discussion, although it defies precise definition. In this part of the book I intend to bring out the basic elements in faith that can effect a change in your life. Faith in God, through Jesus Christ, produces the same overwhelming results among people of any nationality, race, or calling. I urge you, therefore, to cleanse your mind of any wrong teaching that claims faith to become more effective in certain lands than elsewhere. That is the devil's lie! I have seen the Bible work in my life, as in the lives of many others, and I assure you today that a similar change can come to you as you act on God's Word of faith.

Faith can change your destiny! The common denominator among great men of God, servants of God who have seen lasting changes in their lives, has always been *faith* in God. This is evident from many biographies and autobiographies of the great men of God. The story of Smith Wigglesworth, for example, leaves one in no doubt that faith can change your destiny.

Lifted to higher ground

Smith Wigglesworth was a plumber. But he believed with all his heart that he should obey Jesus' instruction in Mark 11:22, 'Have faith in God.' Smith Wigglesworth accepted the call of God—and a new man emerged. My friend, faith in God lifts you to higher ground wherever you may be and whatever God calls you to do. Faith in God to change your destiny always works for the good.

The story of Benin City, Nigeria, has been told many times. Now that the city is prosperous, many have forgotten what it used to represent. To call it dreadful would be an understatement. Suffice to say, it was an unlikely place for God, by man's calculations, to manifest Himself in signs, wonders and miracles. God looked for a man of faith, a man who would act for Him in faith and help to overthrow the powers of darkness. I never imagined it could be me as every morning I pinned my tie, put on my well-ironed trousers and laced my shining shoes. My executive position at the Bata shoe company held great prospects for me. I was popular with the management and was confident that, with hard work and perseverance, the world was my oyster.

Gradually it dawned on me that the tempo of my ministry was increasing. A decision had to be made. Life is full of choices, but faith in God will affect them all, for Christ can do all things. I knew that I was at a crossroads. I had either to hold on to my promising career as a Bata executive, or to launch out by faith into the Master's vineyard. Praise the Lord that by His grace I opted to serve God in full-time ministry. I have never regretted my decision.

All through life there are moments when you are called to lift up your faith to God through Christ. If you do so, you will never be ashamed. Faith can change your destiny, and meanwhile the vision God gives to you will keep you moving forward. Think about this. I believe it takes faith to bring a vision to fruition. Faith and vision are linked.

God's plan for Joseph gives us a clue as to how faith can change one's destiny. His life is a puzzle, full of lessons about the hand of God in the life of a man destined for greatness. It tells of a young man who refused to die before the vision God had given him became a reality. God had a great plan for Joseph, hidden in the distant future. Joseph could not forget that impressive dream of the glorious future which God had scheduled in his timetable. Yet when he told his father and brothers about it (Gen 37), they seemed resentful of the drama. Imagine how Joseph must have spent time musing on his dream. Humanly speaking he did not know how God was going to bring His great promises to pass, but he had faith that somehow they would be fulfilled.

Sometimes when men become aware of God's favour upon you they plot to destroy God's goal for your life; but in almost all cases their schemes only enhance the Master's plan. Envy, treachery and machinations flow from the hearts of men blind with jealousy as they struggle to abort God's plan for His servants. But they always fail. The brothers of Joseph were hell-bent on destroying him. The Bible declares in Genesis 37:26–28 that they sold him to the Ishmaelites who were going to Egypt. It is interesting: as you look back to verse 24 you find out that they had cast Joseph into a pit. Joseph had dreamt that exactly that would happen to him! Did the cruelty of his brothers put

God's plan out of action? Of course not: God was still in control!

Even as a small boy, as he lay there in the muddy pit, Joseph's faith remained steadfast. If the dream is from God and you will only remain constant in faith, then what He has said will be fulfilled. The Ishmaelites bundled Joseph off to Egypt, having no idea of how precious he was to God. Joseph's tribulations were beginning to gather momentum. '*When* will this dream God showed me come to pass?' Joseph might have wondered, as he stood, sadly, behind the prison bars in Potiphar's house. Your belief that faith can change your destiny will be tested and tried. Joseph's faith was tested too, but he kept his eyes on the glory God had revealed to him; even the seducing talks of an enchantress like Potiphar's wife could not throw him off balance. Joseph was determined; he had made up his mind to stand firm. 'But the Lord was with him, and that which he did, the Lord made it to prosper,' (Gen 39:21–23). God was with Joseph, even in prison: the God Who showed the dream to Joseph did not desert him—because he demonstrated faith regardless of circumstances.

Never despair

Many believers miss the blessings of God because they allow despair and temporary distractions to water down their faith in God. Just hold on to Him! Paul gave Timothy the same advice in 2 Timothy 1:12, 'For which cause I also suffer these things, nevertheless I am not ashamed; for I know whom I have believed, and am persuaded that he is able to keep that which I have committed unto him against that day.' Joseph's vision and dream did not diminish because he was thrown into a pit by his brothers. Likewise, whatever your friends or enemies do to you *must not* affect your faith in God: this is crucial. The fact that Joseph was falsely accused and imprisoned did not distract him from his vision. Joseph's well-grounded faith in God protected him like a suit of armour. Faithful is He who promises.

The descriptions of Joseph's later days in Egypt make interesting reading. We see him adorned in beautiful, richly-embroidered clothes as ruler of the country. Men, women and children of all backgrounds bowed to him. He had power and authority over all Egypt. Glance back and see him lying helpless in the pit, refusing to die. Take a look at him behind prison bars, trusting God to put things right. Joseph would soon have been dead, buried and forgotten if he had yielded to doubt, fear and unbelief. The only reason for the change in his destiny was his immovable faith in God.

Through the faith and obedience of one man, Joseph, God fulfilled a great vision. It was not only Joseph's destiny that was changed; the vision touched people and generations as yet unborn. With good reason he was able to tell his brothers, 'And God sent me before you to preserve you a posterity in the earth and to save your lives by a great deliverance' (Gen 45:7). Faith can change your destiny, my friend. Stand up and act in positive faith towards God, hold on even when life seems to be falling apart.

Chapter Six

A VISION FULFILLED

And now these three remain: faith, hope and love.

1 Corinthians 13.13

Many years ago, very early in my ministry, I heard a man remark, 'Without faith, a person's life is filled with dreary failures.' It took me some time to appreciate the wisdom in that saying. Faith is a magnetic word for those who understand what it means. Lack of faith results in diverse negative influences on a man. A man without faith may look on his fellows with downright suspicion and distrust: the basic comfort and assurance of real friendship is lost. Worse still, we may even begin to think that the whole world is against us. Then, gradually, the joy of living begins to wear off.

As a preacher of the Word for well over twenty-five years, across some eighty countries around the world, I have seen that when men lose faith they lose their great ideals and their sense of purpose. Instead, they become obsessed with a sickening 'what's-the-use?' attitude. One man defined faith as 'to continue to believe in certain truths no matter what happens', and steadfastness is an integral part of the faith walk with God. One of the grandest statements in the Bible is Paul's 'I have kept the faith.' He also wrote, 'Now abideth faith...'; meaning that no matter what else happens, faith will last.

A great American preacher has pointed out that the real

profanity of man is not in the use of a few swear words. The most profane word that can pass our lips is the word 'hopeless.' Whenever you say a particular situation or person is hopeless, you are slamming the door in the face of God. There is no such thing as a hopeless situation or person. We are not to give up; tenacity of purpose yields fruits. All you need to back your faith in God is a bit of perseverance and patience.

Abiding faith

Paul's writings to the Corinthians make good reading and my own favourite verse is 1 Corinthians 13:13, 'And now abideth faith, hope, and love, these three'. 'Abideth' means remaining consistent. Over the years of preaching the gospel, I have heard some unbelieving people make such comments as 'Faith is a risky business.' So 'blessed assurance' becomes 'blessed insurance'! The faith which transforms lives and brings visible change is one that believes God is working among us and not just watching us from afar.

The Miracle Centre in Benin City is now documented as the sixth largest church in the world, according to John N. Vanghan's book *The World's Twenty Largest Churches*. I have pastored this church for many years and have preached on faith time and time again. On occasions I have been grieved to see some members of the church unable to launch out to God in faith. Over the lawn I will hear the occasional negative remark, 'This situation is hopeless, I feel like giving up.' My frank reply has always been this: 'Quitters never win, and winners never quit.' In time,

God will reveal His will to us through the workings of divine providence. I know what I am talking about because He has done so in my own life and call to the ministry. You must get it established in your mind that whichever way God reveals His will in your life to perform a particular act, your response must be based on nothing else but faith.

Schweitzer's choice

Have you ever read about Albert Schweitzer? He is considered by many to be one of the great Christians of all time: this had something to do with his faith in God, which ultimately changed his life and consequently his destiny. The moment came when Albert Schweitzer had to decide upon the subject of his life's work. That moment comes for every man and woman at least once in a lifetime. Schweitzer was known to be an exceptionally brilliant young man. His problem was that he had so many abilities —in medicine, music, teaching—and today he is considered a master in each of those fields.

Countless opportunities cross your path, but each life-changing decision must be based on faith in God. What should you do? What must be your stand? One day, Schweitzer was tidying his desk. Among the discarded papers was a little yellow magazine from the Paris Missionary Society. It was addressed, in fact, to a neighbour, but had been put in his mailbox by mistake. It was all part of God's plan. Glancing through it, Schweitzer noticed an article entitled, 'The Needs of the Congo Mission.' Over and over again he read the article and then it began to dawn on him—God was calling him to Africa.

Schweitzer had easily achieved world-wide distinction in theology and music and gone on to earn a doctorate in medicine. He had also served as assistant minister in a busy parish and become a skilled interpreter of the organ music of Bach.

Some people draw a dividing line between faith and intellect, but not Schweitzer, despite all his education. Faith does not suspend our sense of good judgment, it reinforces it. His friends regarded his decision to go and work in Africa as professional suicide. But soon he became more well-known through his work in Africa than he would have been if he had held on to a wealthy clientele in any famous clinic or concert hall. Was it just an accident that the postman put that little magazine in the wrong letter-box? Was it mere chance that it lay unnoticed until the timely moment when Dr Schweitzer's mind was ready to receive direction?

Many people don't respond to God when they ought to because they find it hard to discern His involvement in daily events. Open up by faith today and believe that, as the famous hymn-writer wrote, 'God moves in a mysterious way.' Dr Schweitzer might have sat comfortably in his office and decided that he would lose too much by going to Africa. Thank God, he did not. He was willing to thrust out in faith to God, and his destiny was changed. Through faith we know God has worked out a better purpose for us. If you will only read carefully Hebrews 11, you will know that faith can change your destiny. Read Hebrews 11:16, 'But now they desire a better country, that is, heavenly; wherefore God is not ashamed to be called their God: for he hath prepared for them a city.' Faith makes us desire better things of God according to His promise.

Special words from God

Faith changed my destiny. Today, in response to God's unfolding plan in my life, I have launched out in faith. God told me, 'I the Lord will open a door in the United Kingdom for you to preach My Name among the English' and I believed Him. Believing God's word at the moment when you read it or when it comes into your heart, makes a world of difference later. Some hear through one ear and it passes out through the other ear. Some take it into their heart and allow it to die in their mind. You need to hear, believe and act upon the Word; the revealed Word of God in your heart. Confess it, respect it, because God's Word (according to Isaiah 55.11), 'shall not return unto me void, but it shall accomplish that which I please, and it shall prosper in the thing whereto I sent it.'

It was seven years ago, in Benin City, that I heard God's special instruction to me: He woke me up one cold night, and I sat wrapped in my coverings at the edge of the bed. As I sat there, I could sense the Spirit of God ministering in my heart about the United Kingdom. As far as I could see, there was no knowing as to how the Lord was going to accomplish this feat, but I nevertheless believed Him. I realise that is where the trouble emerges for many Christians. Settle the issue in your mind, move it down to your heart and all will be well. 'Lord,' I prayed, 'I have no funds to make such a grand outreach to the United Kingdom.' Then God spoke back confidently to me, 'I the Lord Who called you will open the doors, I will provide the passage and you will preach my Name.' All to myself, I shouted an affirmative, 'Amen' and 'Alleluia'.

It was still dark, the clock by my bed continued to tick obediently; it was 2.00 am. Looking over towards my wife, I could see she was still in deep sleep. Slowly I stretched my body on to the bed and went back to sleep. But God had not said His last word yet on this United Kingdom outreach. I had a dream. There I was in London. Before me were beautiful buildings, carefully-mown lawns and sleek cars. As I kept walking, I saw thousands upon thousands of people moving in all directions. Suddenly my eyes alighted on a grand-looking five-star hotel, and I felt compelled to walk towards it. Within the precincts of this charming place I was accosted by a handsome-looking man who stretched his hand familiarly to me, 'Welcome, we have been expecting you.' I was so taken aback by the warm reception and the glamour of the surroundings that I forgot to reply.

Then I followed the man along corridor after corridor, until we stopped in a very spacious and magnificent parlour. I was beckoned to take my seat. Everything there was of the very best. As I settled down I began to notice something else. The interior decorations of the parlour were all in red. And the room glittered gloriously as the lights came on. The waiters who attended me were in red attire to match their surroundings. It was breathtaking. 'What can we offer you, sir?' the handsome English waiter asked me. Before I could reply, he gave me a long list of all that was available. I sighed. With care, I placed my order; and when it finally arrived I was satisfied with everything.

After the meal, a courteous official appeared, picked up my bag, paid the bill and ushered me out. I had the full red-carpet treatment. I pondered over this impressive dream for many days. I could not get it out of my mind.

The years passed by, and I went round the globe preaching the Gospel of salvation through Jesus Christ. Invitations swarmed into my office from every continent on earth. I often had to turn down invitations. My tight schedule at home and abroad was bursting at the seams. I went to Australia in 1979. Then to the United States of America. I travelled to the Far East, to present the good news of Jesus to the Malaysians. Europe called and I answered, and so with other African countries and others in North America.

One day I looked through my passport and examined the stamps of various countries, collected as I visited these countries to preach the Gospel. I had been to more than seventy-five countries to proclaim the Risen Christ. Yet that vision and dream of seven years ago had not come to pass; but my faith in God remained as resolute as before.

Vision fulfilled

At the end of 1984 I received a letter with a British postmark. It was from the Reverend Wynne Lewis of Kensington Temple in London. 'We have read your book *Fire In His Bones*' he wrote, 'and have heard all that God has been doing through you around the world. Would you be able to come over to Britain in May 1985 and minister to us?' Great Britain had called me at last! 'I will come,' was my immediate reply.

I went to London in May 1985; a journey that was to be the fulfilment of a dream and a vision of seven years' standing. A high-powered delegation of Pentecostal leaders welcomed me at Heathrow Airport and drove me to a first-class hotel in central London. 'This is a familiar place,' I said to myself as the door of the car was flung open for me to alight. The smooth lawn reminded me of a place I had visited before. I tried to think where and when.

Lifting up my eyes, I surveyed the immaculate edifice of the hotel as we walked into the reception hall. As we walked through the corridors and went up in the lift, it hit me with renewed intensity: 'I have been here before—but when?' A massive glass door opened before me, as my hosts led the way forward. A shining red carpet heralded our arrival. The walls were laced with exquisite decorations of the finest quality. I stood speechless. A steward arrived, spotlessly dressed. He positioned himself near me and said courteously, 'We have been expecting you, sir, what can we offer you?'

In a split second the curtain within my mind was swept back and I recalled my dream and vision. To the minutest detail, the Lord had fulfilled it. It may have taken several years, but time could not change the Master's plan for my life. Nothing can alter what God has set out to do. My dear friend, if you will only believe in your heart and accept the truth that faith in God can bring your dreams to pass, you will be so much happier. Through faith I believe God's Word. Through faith I know He is faithful.

Trials and tribulations could not take away Joseph's dream, neither could they erase mine. Faith can change your destiny. I assure you now that as you place your faith in Christ new visions will take shape in your life, some of them far beyond anything you could imagine. Praise the Lord!

Chapter Seven

A ROOF-TOP DRAMA

Anyone who comes to him must believe that he exists and that he rewards those who earnestly seek him.

Hebrews 11:6

Faith in Christ can make you an achiever. Faith in Christ can make you a goal-setter and a go-getter. Faith in Christ can bring you the best in this life and beyond. Believe me, faith in God through Christ can place you where you want to be. Let me explain the title of this book, *Faith can change your Destiny*.

When I speak of destiny it is both in the sense of its short-term and its long-term meaning. In the short term, faith can change situations and circumstances here on earth: 'Change your position and God will change your situation!' Changing your position means turning from unbelief and doubt to a new position of faith in God's Word. Then as you stand upon the Word in faith, God begins to honour His Word and long-term changes emerge. Many Christians take faith for granted and it is not surprising that different connotations have become attached to the precious Word. But does that affect God's intended meaning of faith? No! Faith remains just as God said.

God created faith and intended that through the exercising of faith, life's best opportunities will be harnessed and fully used for the common good of man. So then if faith can change your destiny for the better, you need also to understand that doubt and unbelief can ruin your destiny. One of the great mysteries of human life is the mystery of cause and effect. Ceaselessly we ask, 'Why this, why that? Why physical sickness? Why afflictions? Why fear and disappointment?' Your faith in Christ can reverse all these.

God has made great and grand provisions for our life span here on earth. Love brings life's fullest blessings but in the same vein it also brings life's hardest pains. Only faith in Christ can reverse that because the Bible says, 'Thou wilt keep him in perfect peace, whose mind is stayed on thee: because he trusteth in thee' (Is 26:3). Why do people commit suicide? They go and hang themselves because they have nothing to hold on to; but we know that faith in Christ will help us to survive any difficult circumstance or crisis. Christ solves crises.

Christ can change things

God has given us the capacity to dream, hope and aspire to life's highest ideals. Sadly, our dreams do not always materialise, our hopes are dashed and despair sets in. In order to make success a possibility we must be willing to accept the responsibility for failure. At the same time you must establish deep in your heart the belief that faith in Christ can turn things around and set you on the way to success.

You may have experienced these things I am writing about now. Your hour of change may have arrived. Life is so full of possibilities; they come in pairs: good and evil, short and tall, black and white, pain and pleasure. You have known that the existence of one carried with it the shadow of the other. Now we come to unravel the mystery. Why then does God seem to intervene for certain individuals and not for others? It is God's wish to set you on the pathway of success and glory, if only you will place your faith where it has to be—in Christ. God gave these words to His people: 'Beloved, I wish above all things that thou mayest prosper and be in health, even as thy soul prospereth' (3 Jn 2). Without faith it is absolutely impossible to please Him and have your needs met, but with faith it is possible to please Him and have situations changed.

Faith in Christ changes things, even though it might seem impossible. The undoing of many people is that they put faith in anything except God and so conditions remain static. They try every known medical breakthrough, but cannot exercise simple faith in God and so little progress is made. For some it is worse than that. I read somewhere a survey which said nine out of ten people on planet earth have no definite plan in life. That is sad indeed.

Faith to move your mountain

In my last book, *Power for your Zero Hour,* we studied the story of the paralysed man as recorded in Luke 5:17–26. We are now going to look at the story as recorded in Mark's gospel (Mk 2:1–12), because there are valuable truths hidden within these verses too.

The first verse shows that Jesus came to Capernaum for an evangelistic outreach and His presence drew the attention of the general public, '. . . it was noised abroad.' The second verse informs us that many gathered to hear Jesus Christ teach and preach and to witness how He healed. People came from far and near; by today's standards they might have come by Concorde, Boeing 747, helicopter, train and car! Among the crowd were religious sightseers, sceptics, cynics, doubters, sincere enquirers, nominal Christians and believers of all shades. They were together in that place to listen to Jesus Christ. The Bible states clearly that before long '. . . there was no room to receive them, no not so much as about the door. . .' (verse 2). There were some, no doubt, who could not endure the pushing and shoving: their best option was to turn round and head for home. 'Maybe some other time I can come and see Jesus; but I cannot stand this crowd today', they might have murmured as they set off for home. The paralytic man heard of Jesus Christ when He visited Capernaum. Six things happened in his life that, ultimately, changed his destiny.

1. He was borne of four men

This paralytic man was down and out. To society he was worthless and useless. But he had one thing that many educated people don't have today: he had faith. Though he could not walk, he knew faith could make a difference. He did not cast away his confidence. What was his destiny? What is the destiny of a paralytic? He was the object of sympathy and pity. He might never be an achiever. Maybe he would not be able to marry or raise a family of his own. As if that was not enough, he was also, probably, a target for scorn and ridicule.

One day a friend visited him. 'Jesus is in town,' he mentioned in passing. 'Who is this Jesus?' the paralytic asked. 'He is the man who teaches, preaches and heals the sick,' the man replied absent-mindedly. And so faith began to be built up in the heart of this man with palsy; he had implicit childlike faith in God and what Jesus can do. 'Could you please take me to where Jesus Christ is ministering?' the paralytic pleaded. Four friends agreed to carry him to the place.

Your friends may say that you have been made for failure and defeat. Ignore them! Listen only to the Word of God, Who tells you that 'if thou canst believe, all things are possible to him that believeth' (Mk 9:23). Accept the challenge, believe the story of faith, and you will be on your way to new heights.

2. *They uncovered the roof where He was*

Four hefty men carried the paralysed man and arrived safely at the place where Jesus was ministering. The crowd was in excess of anything they had expected. Hope seemed faint. The Bible says, '. . . . they could not come nigh unto Him for the press. . . .' (Mk 2:4a). All entry points into the presence of Jesus Christ were barred by the crowd. And after all, who was going to be willing to give way to a man with palsy, when everyone there had a need of some kind or other.

The faith exhibited in this dramatic account is worth emulation. Until a man *really* wants to be rid of his handicap, he will never lose it. Although the four men

71

acted as friends, it was the paralytic who needed healing and therefore a great deal depended on his attitude. 'Shall we take you back home?' the four men might have asked him when they saw the crowd. 'No, I must see Jesus, whatever happens,' the paralytic would have fired back at them. The four men examined the building and made a quick decision. 'Then we shall have to lower you through the roof into the presence of Jesus, if you will agree to that.' 'Yes, of course,' the paralytic replied. And so the stage was set for an adventure of faith. Jesus was no more a mere name. He became a *person* to the paralytic—One who could change his destiny. One who could break through his darkness with the full force of the noonday sun; One who could give back his life, his precious health. All other ideas faded; there was no fear or doubt because his mind was filled entirely with Christ.

The four men lifted the paralytic man across the wall on to the roof-top. 'You people must be crazy!' someone standing down below might have exclaimed. Many of the actions you will have to embark upon as a step of faith may appear stupid to others, but God will honour them. The men were determined. They did not have to go and write a letter to the house-owner, seeking permission to rip off the roof. They had come so far by faith that they would not allow any other obstacle to hinder them. The Bible says '. . . . they let down the bed wherein the sick of the palsy lay' (verse 4b). That was the best they could do. The four men knew the power to heal was not available to them, but they had enough faith to bring the sick to one who could do the healing. Jesus certainly must have heard what was happening on the roof-top. But He would only have looked up and smiled with compassion.

72

The paralysed man was at last within reach of Jesus. My friend, determine in your heart and mind today that Christ must be reached. Know that you will be able to reach Him as you press your way through. The Word of God declares, 'He that cometh to God must believe that he is, and that he is a rewarder of them that diligently seek Him' (Heb 11:6). Beloved, prepare today to raise the roof for victory, raise the roof and see a change of destiny. Dare to go one more mile! Dare to go beyond the conventional, toss overboard pride and the fear of ridicule, move on in boldness and go for your healing. Go for your miracle; it is within reach, so don't let the crowd stop you.

3. Jesus saw their faith

These five simple words made a world of difference. The faith Jesus saw might not have been noticed by other men. If they saw it at all, the possibility is that it could have been misconstrued for foolishness. But thank God for Jesus Christ, Who 'saw their faith.' Faith had brought them away from home on a mission that seemed impossible! Faith made them go one more mile. Faith told them not to go back despite the crowd. It was this daring faith which made them climb the roof and tear it away so that they could meet Jesus. In faith is the victory. Pray to God for this kind of faith: you need it! Faith is a fighter! That is why faith says 'where there is a will there is a way.'

The faith partners had done the best they could and their faith mission was over. It was now up to the paralysed man to take over from where they had left off. There is a stretch of your faith walk that you must walk all alone—

you must believe. You must act on your own.

4. *Son, thy sins be forgiven thee*

These were the first words Jesus spoke to the paralytic
man, 'Son, thy sins be forgiven thee' (verse 5b). Oh, what
a joy it must have been when Jesus called the sick man
'son'. The love of Jesus transcends tribal groupings, it
takes no notice of colour or race. 'Come unto me *all* ye that
labour and are heavy laden and I will give you rest' (Mat
11:28). The healing which Jesus performs within the
sinner at conversion takes place at three levels: body, soul
and spirit. Jesus offered the paralytic the greatest miracle
of all in the Bible—forgiveness of sins (Jn 3:16). His
touching words of forgiveness were an act of grace. You
cannot be healed without receiving a blessing for your
soul.

5. *Arise, take up thy bed, and go thy way into thine house*

This was the one great moment every sick man waits for.
And for the paralytic man it was a dream come true. Jesus
looked him in the face and said gently, 'Arise, take up thy
bed, and go thy way into thine house' (verse 11). The
moment had come for the paralysed man to have a personal
faith, to cut off every connection with the affliction and
actually believe *now* for healing and deliverance. This was a
chance he could not let slip by. Others had told him about
the Master, Who could preach, teach and heal. Others,
out of selfless love, had brought him to the healing service

—but that was not enough. Faith accomplishes things only as it is released; it must be exercised.

For many years, probably, the palsied man had been confined to bed. His limbs were stiff. But I believe Jesus knew all this before He said, 'Arise, take up thy bed.' Jesus will not ask you to do something He knows is absolutely beyond your capacity. The man's faith had to act instantly. And so must your faith arise as soon as it is called for. Faith must first go up, reach out to God and then come down to men. As you read this story, come along, let your faith arise, your miracle is near. Faith requires action on the part of the sick and afflicted. Jesus was saying, 'Arise!' That is a key word. Arise in the inner man first. The inner man stirring up inside helps the outer man draw new vigour and strength into the body.

Today is your day to arise. You must act against the situation or sickness. Take a step of faith, because 'if you change your position, God will change the situation.' The prodigal son arose. He said 'Devil, enough is enough, I am changing my position so that God can change my situation.' It worked for the beggarly prodigal son. It worked for the man with palsy. It worked for the man who had been by the pool of Bethesda for thirty-eight years. I say it will work for you. Arise!

6. *He arose, took up the bed and went before them*

The man with palsy arose. Hallelujah to the King and Lord of lords! If you too will obey His voice in believing faith you will also be able to arise. The crowd was astonished because the man had done the impossible. Why? Because he had faith. Faith can change your destiny too. There are no chains, no fetters, no bonds that faith cannot break. I know of no dark dungeon that faith in Christ cannot light up. I know of no disease that faith in Christ cannot heal. Faith is a fighter and faith in Christ is a winner. Praise the Lord. Faith grants you direct entry into divine blessing, divine abundance and divine love.

The palsied man was healed when he believed the words Jesus spoke. He took up his bed as Jesus had told him. The eternal secret of deliverance is instant obedience. Please take a look at the next few words of verse 12: 'the man went forth before them all; insomuch that they were all amazed.' Who went forth before them all? The healed man who was carried to the healing service exhibited the glory of God before all the crowd. Just think about the beauty of the miracle. He came in through the roof and went out through the door. The crowd would not allow him to see Jesus when he came as a sick man, but they gave him a salute when he walked out whole and healthy. This is a beautiful illustration of 'the first shall be last, and the last shall be first.' But the crux of the matter is that it takes faith in Christ to accomplish such a feat.

Let us take another look at the drama. Shouting is heard all over the place—the paralysed man has been healed by Christ. The crowd jump and dance with excitement; they had seen a living miracle right before their eyes. The healed man begins to walk out, carrying his bed, and someone volunteers to clear the way for him. 'Hey, clear off the path,' a self-appointed escort will shout at the top of his voice. Suddenly everyone can see the healed man and all the crowd wave and clap. Some shake his hands to congratulate him, others take down his address and want to be friends. I love the words Mark recorded in the last part of verse 12, '. . . . and glorified God.' Your sickness does not glorify God. Your doubt and fear do not glorify God. Your poverty and affliction do not glorify God in any way at all. Read what glorifies God and do it. Are you ready to let God be glorified through your life? Then act in faith towards Him. Get out of the bondage and believe Him for the impossible.

The crowd were able to review the whole event and sum it up, '. . . . saying, We never saw it in this fashion' (verse 12b). It was true they had never seen it 'in this fashion.' There is a whole lot of meaning to that small verse. It was not Jesus' first healing miracle; He had been preaching, teaching and healing in several places. Everywhere He was followed by huge crowds. What had so much impressed the Capernaum crowd about the healing of the paralysed man? What so moved them to admit, 'we never saw it in this fashion'? They were more impressed by this singular outstanding miracle than they were with all the dogmatic, ritualistic and boring church services they had ever attended. What they were seeing was not a circus show, it was a faith-healing service. They saw the power of God at work.

Time for action

Will you sit sorrowfully by while Satan is busy destroying your life? You too can be healed. Yes, you can! Your faith exercised in Christ can make people marvel and say, 'We have never seen it this way.' This paralysed man was healed through faith in Christ. His destiny was changed. His life was transformed forever. Strike the devil a deadly blow! Do something *now*! Raise the roof of victory! Cause a ripple! Change the situation through faith in Jesus. God is well able to do it for you!

Chapter Eight

FROM HINDSIGHT TO FORESIGHT

Forgetting what is behind and straining towards what is ahead, I press on towards the goal to win the prize for which God has called me heavenwards in Christ Jesus.

Philippians 3:13

The first step towards a calm confidence in the future is to learn to believe that life is good. That comes from having faith in a God Who you know has the future in His hands as well as your life. God is a *big* God, and expressed faith in Him results in big achievements for you. The real trouble with a lot of people is that their God is too small. They have limited Him. But what did the great Apostle Paul say? 'My God shall supply all your need' (Phil 4:19). What Paul meant was that this God is a big God.

Past, present and future

Many people have no concern about yesterday—after all, it is gone. Others busy their lives thinking about past misfortunes; the records show that such people never get far into the future. Like ostriches they bury their heads— unwilling to look at the present or the future. I firmly believe that when our lives are in harmony with God's will through our faith we have that instinctive sense of the right direction which is the Holy Spirit's guidance, even though we cannot see the way ahead. This is because, 'Thy word is a lamp unto my feet, and a light unto my path.'

The journey of life into the future must be travelled one step at a time. The Bible says that for every single step God sheds His glorious light on our path. All you need to do is keep walking on in unstained fellowship. As we move steadily and fearlessly ahead we know that through the storms and unavoidable uncertainties we shall come to the right place at last. My word to you is this: move on by turning your face toward the dim unknown of tomorrow, believing every step of the way that the hands of the Almighty Christ will cover you. David wrote the great words of Psalm 23: 'Yea, though I walk through the valley of the shadow of death, I will fear no evil: for thou art with me . . .' David knew that there would be valleys ahead. But the word *through* is crucial. You will fear no evil because when you walk *through* it, God will be right there with you. David wrote, 'For thou art with me.' When your whole life is centred in God, He will be there through the good and bad times. You will know that somehow, through faith in Him, all things will work out fine. And with that faith we can say, like Tennyson, 'The mighty hopes of faith make us men.' Faith in God's Word will remind you of Proverbs 13:12: 'Hope deferred maketh the heart sick, but when the desire cometh, it is a tree of life.'

Faith is mentioned more and more in the New Testament because it is a new covenant book, wherein 'the just shall live by faith'. It is saddening that thousands of Christians are spending their precious lives believing the devil's lie. On the verge of tears, they will say 'I have no faith, I can't make it!' They depend on other people's faith for their miracles. It is time you acted on God's Word and saw your own miracle! Every Christian has equal rights, and it is

God's will and His heart's desire that each one of His children learns how to avail himself of all His blessings. Believe the words you are hearing, act upon them, and see your mustard seed faith develop into an oak tree miracle in every area of your life.

Faith that works

Jesus left behind for all His followers, the key to God's storehouse. He said, 'Have faith in God. For verily I say unto you, That whosoever shall say unto this mountain, Be thou removed, and be thou cast into the sea, and shall not doubt in his heart, but shall believe that those things which he saith shall come to pass; he shall have whatsoever he saith' (Mk 11:22, 23). If your understanding of faith is to be renewed then you must sit down and re-examine these verses.

Jesus emphasised '*Have faith in God*' (Mk 11:22). It will not surprise you to hear that this verse was among the collection I learnt very soon after my conversion and the glamour of it has not been lost with the years. If anything I have come to appreciate even more the secret of having deep-seated faith in God. Jesus said 'Have faith *in God*'—not in ourselves, our friends, occult powers, secret societies or the mastermind of evil, Satan. The Lord said 'Have faith in God.' The reason is simple. Faith in God the Creator works much more effectively than faith in any form of His creation. The exhortation of Jesus for us to have faith in God is followed by another powerful word in Scripture. 'For verily . . . whosoever [that strictly means *any* person; me as well as you] says unto this mountain . . . ' Notice that faith here is straightforward, specific and definite.

I want to issue a challenge to you at this point. Select any circumstance of your own life where there is a blockage and I assure you with all my heart as a servant of the living God that this formula will apply. 'Be thou removed'...means just that—taken out of the way. The stumbling-block or barrier to your dream, vision or goal is removed by faith in God. The devil, according to the Bible, is a deceiver, a liar and a traitor, sometimes disguised as an angel of light. Don't allow him to bring unbelief and doubt into your life. The next part of the Scripture we are exploring says that all barriers to faith are 'cast into the sea'—that is, gone forever. The hindrance and blockage is gone, complete victory lies in wait, so move on further by faith.

In Mark 11:23, two important words stand face to face with each other—doubt and belief. To move forward in faith you must conquer doubt at all costs, knowing that God is true (Rom 3:4a) and that He will keep His word regardless of what doubt says. Please understand this, because many other things revolve around this pivot. As soon as you settle the matter of doubt you are on your way to new heights of faith through believing His word. It is through your personal faith that victory will be accomplished.

God never gives up

I repeat: faith *can* change your destiny. It worked for me in Africa, so it can work for you in England or America or India. The same unchangeable God reigns and rules over the whole universe. Any deficiencies are within our faith, and that is why we must tune it like an engine and overhaul it with the Word of God which endureth forever and is able to quicken and renew. You cannot have faith in God without knowledge of His word (see again Mk 11:22–23). Yet some will shrug their shoulders and say, 'It is not true, I don't believe it.' Their unbelief, however, will not alter the everlasting Word of glory. It is futile to contradict the most reliable book in the whole world. If you say 'I don't believe in the power of faith,' you are coming against the testimony of the best in today's modern science. Science declares boldly that 'video recorders work' and for that reason the man who spends money on one has faith that it will work and then sees it work. Both Christ and science say 'faith works' and as you believe and act in faith you see the result.

A second attitude towards the power of faith is also very common and this is, 'I do not understand it; it is beyond me.' That is neither here nor there! It is no use sitting on the fence: you either believe or you do not. Many people, including millions of professional Christians, daily claim that they are 'managing'. For how long will you 'manage'? Now is the time to direct your faith to God and see yourself a master of the crisis that is rocking you. You may give up and cry 'I can't do it,' but that is defeatist. God never gives up on a man—neither must you give up on your situation. Paul told us to 'fight the good fight of faith.' Develop your faith, build upon it, experience it. Even as you read this, I urge you to believe that God's power is being released in your life. Place your entire faith in Him now!

The battle royal

Writing in *International Gospel News*, Howard T. Lewis reports that the global population is growing by more than 200,000 a day. Over half have never heard the Gospel. 'The arithmetic of population growth is awesome and sobering,' says the report. 'The earth gains 150 new persons a minute—9,100 per hour—218,100 per day—79.6 million per year. One wonders out of this vast number, how many will ever have the opportunity to learn about the new birth . . . ' These challenging and staggering statistics gave me new vision for the gospel as I studied at the Christ for the Nations College, Dallas, Texas, USA in 1971. 'I cannot go back to Africa and be the same,' I kept impressing upon myself. 'I shall now believe God for a change in the destiny of my people.'

During the entire period of my course, an unexplainable zeal consumed me. I fasted, I prayed, I sought the face of God by even greater crying daily, 'Lord, you promised to send me back to my country with a flame of fire in my soul. Help my people to recognise it and to be willing to follow in the direction you lead me.' It was as if I was gathering speed by an acceleration; the anointing of God increased in no small measure on my life. Then the time came for me to return to my country—Nigeria. Can I ever forget that day? It was incredible. One by one, as various people came to give me a welcome handshake, they were slain in the Spirit—right there on the tarmac! A collection of people were filled instantly with the Holy Spirit and began speaking in tongues. As I turned to grasp another hand being extended, the power of the Holy Spirit came down, until about twenty people had fallen under His power!

There on the tarmac at the Benin City airport the God of miracles showed forth His power and I got the message—a new dawn was breaking! The voice of God kept ringing in my heart, telling me not to lose sight of my vision. From the balcony of my house I looked over the city of Benin. There had not been any change; culture, tradition, religion and dogmatism reigned supreme. Yet I had a vision for my nation, a vision for a heathen people, to point people to the marvellous light of Jesus Christ. Once I woke up in the night and said to myself, 'Now is the accepted time to launch into the deep.' I called together the elders of the small church at Iyaro in the heart of Benin City, and Brother Elton (my spiritual mentor), to discuss a master plan for evangelism. We studied the map of Nigeria and earmarked places and targets. We all agreed that we should begin in our home town of Benin City.

Then an idea came into my mind: 'Why not contact some of the old bishops and ministers in Benin City for their ideas and support in this evangelistic venture?' Little did I know that I was to learn a bitter lesson through this experience. One by one I visited the old bishops and ministers of the orthodox and evangelical churches. I laid bare my heart and vision to each of them. One by one they sat me down. With concern, pity and seriousness they said to me, 'Idahosa, it is impossible. We were here many years before you were born—just take it easy. Nobody will come to such a big crusade!' My heart nearly broke with self-pity and anguish at their attitude. Through my tears and pain I heard the still small voice of God: 'My son Idahosa, Who called you to the ministry?' 'It was you, Lord, Who called me,' I replied. The Lord fired back at me, 'Who gave you the vision?' I repeated my answer, 'You, Lord!' A momentary silence followed and then God said to me, 'Benson, I called you and gave you the vision; trust me and go on. I will provide all that men cannot give you.'

After what seemed like a long dark night, I woke up bubbling with renewed zeal and vigour. I knew a new story was about to unfold. Don't allow anyone to spoil the vison God has embedded in your heart. Believe that God will stand by you, and all will be well. We booked the Ogbe Stadium, Benin City, for the massive crusade to be held in February 1972; it was a historic outreach in faith and success. The Ogbe Stadium seats well over 60,000 and that, by all standards, was beyond the strength of an emerging ministry. But we serve a big God and with Him nothing shall be impossible. We had faith to publicise the crusade on radio. We ran adverts in the papers. We drove a van through the city announcing it. Suspense and expectation filled the air. Only heaven will reveal the impact and dimensions of the Ogbe Stadium crusade of 1972. Thousands of people came night after night; thousands were saved and washed by the Blood of the Lamb.

My faith in God brought success by His grace. The church at Iyara soon spilled over with new converts. Some of them are now senior pastors with me. Very many hundreds have grown in the faith to key positions in the Lord's vineyard. Some are deaconesses, deacons and elders. To God be the glory! Hundreds of the faithful who were converted then have stood by me through the storms and tough times of my ministry. One thing made all the difference, faith in God. Faith can change your destiny, and the destiny of others.

Making full proof of faith

By the grace of God, I have seen faith work more miracles than many will ever be privileged to witness on this earth. I have seen faith in God work in our family, in the church and many other areas of life. Faith has no limit, faith does not recognise any hindrance, faith in God based upon the Word overcomes all stumbling blocks. Faith can change your destiny, *if* you will let it. Will you? My ministry is so full of convincing testimonies to the wonder-working power of faith that today I have no fear as to what it can do. Truly *all* things are possible with God. Even disappointments can be turned into His appointments. It may be hard to believe that Paul's prison was God's appointment. But although Paul saw all that represented the cruelty and wickedness of men, he also managed to turn his disappointment into God's appointment (see 2 Cor 11). Faith in God changes things, no matter how hopeless they may look. Paul followed his own advice to others, 'and having done all, to stand.' He turned his excuses to uses, turning to God for inspiration and aspiration. These are the ingredients of faith.

Paul had dreamed of going one day to Spain. But instead he ended up in a Roman prison! Some would have merely folded their hands, done nothing and wasted away. Others would have cried out to heaven or would have accused God to His face, as Job's unthoughtful friends advised him to do. Paul knew better. He tenaciously dedicated himself to God, even in prison. Later he wrote, 'But I would ye should understand, brethren, that the things which happened unto me have fallen out rather unto the furtherance of the gospel' (Phil 1:12). Paul knew that although he could not get through to the multitudes in Spain, he *would* win the guards in prison. We can learn a lesson from his experience: 'if you cannot have the opportunities you wanted, you can take the opportunities you have.' Paul's prison epistles contain some of his deepest revelations from the treasures of God's wisdom and knowledge. Faith changed the destiny of Paul. Faith can change your destiny too.

Coping with 'failure'

It may well be that, like Paul, you have missed out on something you dreamed of. You might have ended up in a prison of disappointment. Now, if you can't get out of your prison, let God help you make something out of it: faith can change your destiny. Disappointments, failures and trials are the eggs we break to make the omelettes of life's success. Through faith in God, your disappointments can become stepping-stones to greater achievements. Give faith in God a chance. I have shown you how the Apostle Paul recognised that forceful fact. He said boldly, '. . . forgetting those things which are behind . . . reaching forth unto those things which are before' (Phil 3:13). If you will only understand that just as faith overcomes fear, and love conquers hate, so positive action overcomes past failures. Stop keeping company with your failures. Lift high your head, look into tomorrow and let the sky be your limit.

Recently I was involved in a particularly busy schedule at the church where I am a pastor. One day I sank into the sofa to relax, picking up a magazine to glance through. I read an article about a young man who one summer sold books from door to door. He was lame and walked only with great difficulty. At one house a young lady rudely dismissed him. But when he started to walk away, she saw his lameness and out of pity called him back. 'Oh I am sorry, I didn't know you were lame,' she said cheerfully. 'I will buy a book.' The young man wasn't selling sympathy as the lady assumed; he was selling books, and he made no secret of that. Beaten down with shame she said, 'Doesn't being lame direct your life?' The young man answered beautifully, 'Yes, but thanks to God I can choose the direction.' What a lesson for you! When you hear someone say 'Don't give up,' be determined to allow faith one more chance—it may well be the answer.

Prayer

Praying to God from a born-again Christian's point of view is a definite act of faith. Expecting an answer to prayer is an act of faith. Acting on the revelation of God to bring to pass His will is an act of faith. This is the faith which alters situations. This is the faith which changes the destiny of men and women through Jesus Christ our Lord. I don't understand prayer any more than I understand electricity. But I do know that the mysterious power of electricity can be harnessed to do many useful things. Likewise consistent prayer increases our faith, whereas lack of prayer is harmful: 'Seven days without prayer makes one weak!' Prayer is a propeller to faith. It rises up and moves forward to its destination.

Unceasingly people thronged to Jesus to hear Him preach, teach or heal. One day a man came to Christ seeking urgent help for his sick son. Jesus Christ was ready. The man said 'if thou canst do anything, have compassion on us, and help us.' Do you notice where he puts the 'if'? 'If thou canst do anything,' he says. The 'if' of the man is in reference to Christ, but the Lord calmly corrects that and replies 'If *thou canst believe,* all things are possible to him that believeth' (Mk 9:22–23). Better get it clear that the 'if' is not with God; it is with you! Jesus Christ said plainly that the only limit to our prayer is the limit of our own belief: the mental actualisation of the vision, the vision in the mind.

Before a building is begun, the architects draw the plans. And, as Edison once said, 'Science can create anything it can conceive of.' Similarly, faith can create anything it can conceive of. That is what God says. Believing is drawing a mental blueprint and when that is settled the word 'impossible' is eliminated from your thinking. If science says it can conceive and create, then faith declares that it can believe and bring it to pass. In the course of my travels around the world I have seen some of the most magnificent buildings ever designed by man. Sometimes as I look at the grandeur, finesse and elegance of these fabulous works of architecture I say to myself 'God, give me a vision of these great edifices for the expansion of your kingdom in Africa.' Those who have no faith think that God does not answer prayer, but as a man of faith I know He does.

The Faith Centre Miracle

My wife and I were flying from Los Angeles to Sydney when God showed me the vision of a huge auditorium.

'What is this, Lord?' I asked. Then God told me: 'In this building, the words of Life will be proclaimed. Men and women will come from every part of the world to see a demonstration of the power of Jesus Christ to save, heal and deliver. To the glory of My Name.' I was elated and excited because I knew God was going to do something big. Every good and every perfect gift comes from God, in Whom there is no variableness nor shadow of turning.

Almost everyone else was taking a nap, but there I was—plugging in to the powerhouse of God for vision to change the destiny of my people. He began to unfold the design, architecture and blueprint of the building to me. I reached into my bag and grabbed the only piece of paper available—my boarding pass. On the boarding pass I drew the design and plan as revealed by the Lord, for what was to become the biggest Christian auditorium on the continent of Africa. The vision may have been heavenly, but the fulfilment is on the earth.

Finally, at the end of our preaching tour we reached Benin City, Nigeria. I sent for the builder and took him to the site where the building was to be constructed. He was alarmed at the proposed size of the building, which was to seat well over 20,000. I called it the first Gospel Stadium or Stadium Church in the world! When the architect came he just nodded his head as I explained the details from my artwork on the boarding pass. He caught the vision!

The circumference of the Christian Faith Centre Auditorium, now completed, is 886,000 feet—that will give you an idea of the size of my faith and vision. Today in Benin City stands the magnificent edifice of what was only a dream or vision in the sky, high over Los Angeles. Don't lose sight of your vision. Faith made it all possible. Faith can change situations, circumstances and the destinies of men, if only you will believe God's Word and act upon it.

I have attempted to set out some of the spiritual truths coming from a tested and proven faith walk with God. Renew your mind with these lessons and you will never be the same again. Not even the devil can hold you back. Life is similar to mountain climbing in that the climber is always struggling higher. But it is different in that in life we never reach the top. We never arrive because we never run out of heights to climb. But go out and aim for life's highest point, because faith in God through Christ can change your destiny.

Jesus Christ and you!

A sinner's prayer to accept Jesus as Lord and Saviour

Our God and Father in Heaven: I come before Your throne in Jesus' Name. Your Word says that 'All have sinned and come short of the glory of God' (Rom 3: 23), and that 'The wages of sin is death' (Rom 6:23). But You also say in Your Word that, 'Whosoever shall call upon the Name of the Lord shall be saved' (Rom 10:13). I am calling on You to save me now!

You have said, 'If thou shalt confess with thy mouth the Lord Jesus, and shalt believe in thine heart that God hath raised Him from the dead, thou shalt be saved. For with the heart man believeth unto righteousness; and with the mouth confession is made unto salvation' (Rom 10:9–10).

I believe in my heart that Jesus Christ is the Son of God who died for my sins, and that He was raised for my justification. I confess Him now as my Saviour and Lord.

Hallelujah! I have now become the righteousness of God in Christ (2 Cor 5:21)! Praise the Lord, I am saved!

Signed . . . .

Name and address . . . .

. . . .

. . . .

Date . . . .